Eating Problems in Children: Information for Parents

BY C

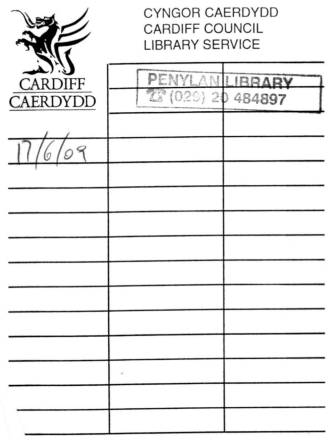

CYNGOR CAERDYDD
CARDIFF COUNCIL
LIBRARY SERVICE

© The Royal College of Psychiatrists 2002.

Gaskell is an imprint of the Royal College of Psychiatrists, 17 Belgrave Square, London SW1X 8PG.

British Library Cataloguing-in-Publication Data
A catalogue record for this book is available from the British Library.

ISBN 1-901242-86-2

Distributed in North America by Balogh International Inc.

Gaskell is a registered trademark of the Royal College of Psychiatrists.

The Royal College of Psychiatrists is a registered charity (no. 228636).
Printed in Great Britain by Henry Ling Limited, The Dorset Press, Dorchester.

Cover artwork © Catherine Brighton, 2001

contents

Preface   v

Acknowledgements   vii

Introduction   viii

1. What types of eating problems do children suffer from?   1
   Identifying eating problems in children   2
   Types of eating problems in children   3
   Eating problems and age groups   10

2. How many children suffer from eating problems?   12
   What do we know?   12
   Is the number of children who suffer from eating
   problems rising?   14

3. What causes eating problems in children?   16
   Why do some children have problems with eating?   16
   Are some children more likely to suffer from eating
   problems than others?   18

4. Who treats children with eating problems?   21
   What types of professionals treat children with eating
   problems?   21
   What about specialist services for children with eating
   problems?   24

5. What type of treatment is available for children with eating
   problems?   26
   To whom should you go to begin with?   26
   What does specialist treatment involve?   27
   What types of treatment are available?   28
   What should I do if my child has...?   34

6. What is the long-term outlook for children with eating
   problems?   41
   What is the outlook for...?   41
   What effect can eating problems have on growth and
   development?   44

7. Need more information?   51
   Useful addresses   51
   Further reading   52

Appendix. How to assess a child's growth potential   53
   Adult height potential   53

Glossary   56

Index   59

preface

Whatever the eating problem – fussiness about food, being frightened of certain foods, difficulty trying new foods, or not eating much at all – it is understandable that problems with a child's eating will cause worry and concern to parents. It is important to find out whether the eating problem is a normal phase in development that the child will grow out of, or whether it is more serious, longer lasting and likely to have an effect on the growth and development of the child.

Parents and carers will be interested in this book for different reasons. They may be at the end of their tether because of the eating behaviour of their child or because they are wondering whether their child's eating patterns are normal or not – and they are worrying about nothing. Whatever the reason, this book aims to provide a source of current and accurate information about eating problems in childhood. The book is mainly concerned with children between the age of 5 and 12 years, but there is not an exact age at which children can suffer from the eating problems described. The book does not discuss issues that relate to infants who suffer from feeding problems, such as failure to thrive (see Glossary), and although eating problems in pre-school children as well as anorexia nervosa and bulimia nervosa are discussed, they are not the focus of this book.

This book begins with a chapter on the different types of eating problems that children can suffer from. The chapter is an important one because it is not clear exactly what types of eating problems are found in children. It is hoped that this chapter will help to clear up some of this confusion. The book then turns to common questions that parents and carers of children with eating problems may have: further chapters discuss how many children suffer from eating problems, what causes eating problems in children, who treats children with eating problems, how the different types of eating problems are treated and what the future holds for children who suffer from eating problems. Chapter 7 provides useful addresses and suggestions for further reading, for readers seeking more information. The Appendix indicates how to assess a child's growth potential, as this may prove useful when determining whether any harm is likely to have arisen as a result of a child's eating problem. Finally, we have included a Glossary to help parents understand some of the jargon that is used when talking about eating problems in children.

acknowledgements

We are grateful to Dr Rachel Bryant-Waugh, Dr Jo Douglas, Dr Bryan Lask and Dr Dasha Nicholls, who provided us with help and advice through their work with children who suffer from eating problems and without whom the completion of this book would not have been possible. We would also like to thank Dr Mike Shooter for his comments on early drafts of this book.

The FOCUS Project is funded by a grant from the Gatsby Charitable Foundation and the Department of Health (Section 64 Grant Award).

The FOCUS Project has tried to ensure that this book is accurate but cannot take responsibility for errors or omissions. The information contained within this book does not necessarily reflect the view of the Royal College of Psychiatrists.

introduction

The majority of children will, at some time in the first five years of their life, have some problems with eating. For example, they may eat only a few different types of food or appear not to eat much at all. For most of these children, this will be a passing phase and they will grow out of it. But for some, the eating problem will be more serious and will last longer.

It has been formally recognised that children can suffer from eating problems only within the past 20 years. There is very little information available about the eating problems that children can suffer from. Most of what we know has come from the experience and expertise of the professionals who treat children with eating problems, and not through evidence based on good research.

The types of eating problems that children suffer from are very different from the eating disorders that teenagers and adults suffer from. They also have different causes and different forms of treatment. Also, children can suffer from more different types of eating problems than do teenagers or adults. Moreover, children suffer from problems with eating before they have finished growing and so such problems can have more of an effect on them physically.

The current lack of knowledge has led to some confusion and debate. There are a number of reasons for this. Firstly, different words are used to describe eating problems in children. The names of the types of eating problems found have come from the professionals who treat them. Different words are used because there are lots of different professionals who treat children with eating problems, for example psychologists, psychiatrists, speech therapists, physiotherapists, nutritionists and dieticians. It is not clear therefore exactly what types of eating problems children can suffer from.

There is also confusion because it is common for pre-school children to have problems with eating. This is seen as a stage of normal development in this age group, when children experiment with new tastes and textures, as well as with the effect that their behaviour has on their parents or carers. In these cases the eating problem should be described as 'a phase', which the child will grow out of. However, eating problems in older children are more serious, for example an eight-year-old child who is fussy about food and will only eat cheese sandwiches, chips, and cheese and tomato pizza (a 'selective eater'), because eating problems are not then appropriate to the child's stage of development. As children grow up, they develop a more sophisticated mental ability, which means that an eating problem may be related to underlying psychological issues.

Lastly, there is confusion because the same words are used to describe different things. For example 'problem' and 'disorder' are used to describe the same conditions. This means that some professionals will refer to children as suffering from eating 'disorders', while others will refer to them as suffering from eating 'problems'. Also, sometimes 'disorder' may be used to show that the eating problem is more serious. Confused? Well, it's not surprising!

Before reading any further, it is important to clear up these difficulties. Within this book, infants and very young children will be referred to as having 'feeding problems'. This is because eating at this time in the child's life is much more interactive and they are 'fed' rather than 'eating' on their own. Children who have problems with their eating will be referred to as having 'eating problems'. We believe that it is important not to describe children as having an 'eating disorder' because this term is mainly used to describe adolescents and adults who have problems with their eating. Adolescents and adults tend to suffer from very different problems from children, so it is important to make this distinction. Although infants, children and adolescents can all suffer from problems with their eating, the problems that they suffer from are very different. In summary, in order to make it clear which age group is being talked about, within this book infants are referred to as suffering from 'feeding problems', children from 'eating problems' and adolescents from 'eating disorders' (see diagram below).

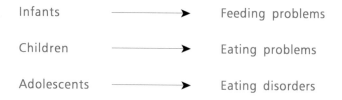

Infants	⟶	Feeding problems
Children	⟶	Eating problems
Adolescents	⟶	Eating disorders

So with this in mind, read on. We hope that you will find useful information about the eating problems that children can suffer from and that the book will help you to find answers to some of the questions that you may have, to help you to know where to get more information from if you need it, and perhaps even to reduce some of the worry that eating problems bring with them.

one what types of eating problems do children suffer from?

The eating patterns of quite a large number of children will cause concern to their parents at some stage, but these are usually just a normal phase in the child's development. For example, it is quite common for most toddlers to go through a phase of being fussy about food. This means that they will eat only a narrow range of foods, perhaps crisps, peanut-butter sandwiches, chicken nuggets and chips, or will drink, say, only milk. Even if children eat a very small number of different types of food, if they are taking in enough calories and nutrients so that they are not hungry and are growing normally, then no harm will come to them. The majority of these children will begin to eat a wider range of foods as they get older.

The term 'eating disorder' is often associated with the tragic stories of young people's deaths from anorexia nervosa that hit the headlines, and it is common to find articles on eating disorders in magazines and newspapers. As a result there are many myths about them, which can be difficult to separate from the facts. Before going any further, it is important to point out that the eating problems that children suffer from are very different to the eating disorders that are found in adolescents and adults. Here are the reasons why:

- There are more different types of eating problems found in children.
- Eating problems in children have different causes.
- They have different characteristics.
- They need different types of treatment.

It is understandable that problems with a child's eating will cause concern and anxiety for parents, as they wonder whether their child is eating too much or too little or getting enough of the right 'sorts' of food. Sometimes a child will pick up on these concerns and this may cause the eating problem to last longer than it otherwise would. As a general rule, therefore, if the child is growing normally and is happy and healthy, then a change in diet should not be a reason to worry. In fact, only a few of the eating problems found in children are really problematic and will affect the growth and development of the child. The majority of children tend to grow out of their eating problem.

IDENTIFYING EATING PROBLEMS IN CHILDREN

Identifying and diagnosing eating problems in children can be harder than you might think. When they are trying to identify a particular condition, professionals will often use a manual that lists the symptoms of different disorders. Identification of the condition will help them to know how the condition will need to be treated. However, childhood eating problems are not included in any of the major diagnostic manuals. This is because eating problems in children have really been recognised by professionals only within the past 20 years. There is consequently still a lot of confusion and disagreement about eating problems in children, because not much is known about them. As a result, professionals from different backgrounds use different words to describe the same eating problem; for example, 'selective eating', 'faddy eating' and 'extreme faddiness' are all used to describe children who eat only a very narrow range of foods. A large number of different terms are used because there are a large number of different professionals who treat children with eating problems, for example doctors, psychologists, psychiatrists, speech therapists, physiotherapists, nutritionists and dieticians.

Because of the difficulty in identifying particular eating problems in children, researchers have tried to develop ways of classifying these conditions. For example, some have divided the problems by the different symptoms, while others have divided them according to cause. There is not a generally accepted way of classifying childhood eating problems. More research is needed so that a good method of classification can be developed, which can then be used to identify the different types of eating problems in children and help with their treatment. The question still remains, though – what types of eating problems do children suffer from?

TYPES OF EATING PROBLEMS IN CHILDREN

Below are a number of case examples that describe children with different types of eating problems. These do not describe real children, but they have been created in order to show the different types of eating problems that are found in children. Note that all of the eating problems described here can occur in either boys or girls. They provide only a general description, as symptoms of a particular eating problem may vary from child to child. Also, a child may have symptoms of more than one eating problem, and this will make it more difficult to diagnose the condition.

Selective eating (extreme faddiness)

> Billy was eight years old when he was referred for treatment. He would eat only marmalade or bacon sandwiches, chips and crisps. Billy had been eating these foods and nothing else for a number of years. When Billy's mother tried to get him to try new foods he got very upset and said that he felt sick. However, Billy had no problem swallowing and keeping down his favourite foods. He was of normal weight and height, as he seemed to get enough calories and nutrients from the food that he did eat. He was doing well at school and had lots of friends. His parents sought help because Billy's selective eating had started to affect his relationships with his friends, as he wouldn't go to his best friend's house for tea and was anxious about going to his friends' birthday parties.

- The most obvious feature of this condition is the narrow range of food that is eaten. This has usually been a problem for at least two years.

- These children are very unwilling to try new types of food.

- The behaviour of these children is usually normal, unless they feel that they are being forced to eat a wider range of foods than they feel comfortable with.

- Problems may start to occur when the child is about eight years old because the selective eating causes difficulties over going to birthday parties or staying at a friend's house.

- Children who eat only a restricted sugary diet may also have problems with their teeth.

- The weight of these children does not give much of an indication as to whether there is a problem – they may be of low, normal or high weight.

Restrictive eating (poor appetite)

David was seven years old and seemed not to eat very much at all. Although he ate a range of different foods, he seemed not to be interested in food. His parents had been worried about the amount that David was eating and went to see their doctor. They were told that David was growing satisfactorily and that he was healthy. David continued to eat very small portions and ate snacks during the day. Although skinny and short for his age, he continued to grow and develop, and had no other emotional problems.

- These children eat smaller amounts of food than they should do for their age.

- Their diet will be normal in terms of the range of food eaten and the nutrients that it contains.

- These children are often thin and their height tends to be low, but otherwise they generally seem healthy.

- It almost seems as if restrictive eaters are 'programmed' to eat less and to be thin but healthy.

- Often, other members of the family will have a history of the same pattern of food intake.

Food phobia

James was nine years old when he was seen for treatment. Six weeks previously he had choked on a piece of popcorn. After this James had refused to eat any solid food and had lost a lot of weight. He would drink only milk and eat only pureed food. He said that he was frightened of eating solid food because he thought that he might choke again and wouldn't be able to breathe.

- These children are usually very resistant to eating and drinking, which can cause a great deal of concern.

- They may avoid foods that have certain textures because they are frightened of swallowing.

- They are usually frightened of choking, gagging or being sick, and some children say that eating and drinking hurts. This means that meals often turn into a battleground.

- Some children may be fearful and anxious of eating new or disliked foods.

- The majority of these children do, however, seem to grow and develop because the food and drink that they will have provide enough calories and nutrients.

Food refusal

Jamie was seen for treatment at the age of six years. Since he had started primary school his teacher had become very worried about him. He had no problem eating the snacks that his mum had given to him for break time and would eat chicken nuggets and chips, his favourite meal, when they were on the school menu, but refused to eat anything else that the school provided. On assessment it was clear that, at home, Jamie had a balanced diet. He was of normal weight and was healthy. It appeared that Jamie was worried and very unhappy at school, and that the eating problem was a way of expressing this.

- Food refusal is commonly found in pre-school children, where the refusal of food can be used as a way to get other things.

- However, this can persist in slightly older children, where the main feature is an inconsistent refusal of food.

- These children will tend to eat their favourite foods without any problem at all.

- They may refuse food only when they are with particular people or in a particular situation – for example, refusing to eat at school but eating normally at home.

- Worry or unhappiness underlies the food refusal in many cases.

- These children are usually of normal weight and height, and this problem does not usually pose a threat to the child's health.

Inappropriate texture of food for age

Lucy was four years old and would eat only pureed or semi-solid food (this would usually be what a six- to ten-month-old infant would eat). When Lucy was given food that had lumps in, she would spit the food out and then refuse to eat altogether. Lucy was not underweight but her parents were concerned about the effect that her condition would have on her when she went to primary school.

- The most obvious sign of this condition is the refusal to eat any solid food that requires biting and chewing.

- These children also tend to spit out the food, gag or refuse to eat it if it contains lumps.

- They may also refuse to eat finger foods.

- The majority of these children tend to be of normal weight, but some may be underweight.

- For older children, difficulties could arise around eating at school.

Food avoidance emotional disorder

Jane was 11 years old when she was seen for treatment and was very pale and thin. After Jane's grandma, a person to whom she had been very close, had died, she had become very sad and tearful and lost her appetite. Her mother had taken her to see their doctor, who referred them to a specialist service, saying that he thought that Jane was suffering from anorexia nervosa. However, on assessment, Jane said that she knew that she was thin and needed to put on weight, but that she just didn't feel hungry. It was clear that she had emotional problems and worries that were interfering with her appetite. Jane was therefore diagnosed as having food avoidance emotional disorder.

- These children often wish that they could eat more and are concerned about being thin.

- The loss of appetite is usually associated with depression or anxiety.

- In food avoidance emotional disorder there is a more general disturbance in behaviour that does not centre on food and mealtimes.

- The child may experience a loss of appetite, problems with sleeping, poor concentration, tearfulness and a general sense of hopelessness.

- These children may actually say that they feel sad, and this sadness can be seen in their posture, the way they move, their facial expression and their tone of voice.

- They also may avoid school and contact with their friends, and want to stay at home.

Childhood-onset anorexia nervosa

At the age of 11, Kirsty announced to her parents that she was going on a diet. Her parents didn't take this too seriously and told her that she didn't need to lose any weight. Kirsty, however, was adamant. She started to go shopping with her mum and insist that she bought low-fat food for her to eat. If her mum refused to buy Kirsty individual low-fat meals, this would cause a lot of shouting and tantrums. Her parents became concerned about her obsession with food and also noticed that she was eating hardly anything at all and had started making negative comments about herself. She now insisted on walking to school and was doing extra activities after school that involved exercise. Although Kirsty had lost a lot of weight, when her parents asked her about this and about the amount of food that she was eating she became very upset, shouting that she was fat, she hated herself and she had to lose more weight.

The telltale signs of anorexia nervosa can be divided into those that are related to food, those that are to do with general mood and behaviour, and those that are physical:

- *Food-related signs* – obsession with food; sensitivity about eating; not eating much at all; wanting to eat alone; choosing only low-calorie foods; hiding food under the table, in serviettes or clothes pockets; collecting and storing food; denying hunger when it is obvious that they are hungry; extreme irritability when meals are earlier or later than usual; eating a lot of salt, vinegar or spicy foods.

- *General behaviour signs* – frequent weighing; excessive exercising; gathering information on dieting from leaflets, books and magazines; wearing baggy clothes; general irritability, especially when questioned about eating; developing rigid daily routines; not wanting to go out with friends any more.

- *Physical features* – weight loss; loss of or failure to start periods; dizziness, sometimes fainting; tiredness; stomach pains and feeling full when only a small amount of food has been eaten; low body temperature and feeling cold; poor blood circulation, leading to cold hands and feet; dull and lifeless hair, which may fall out; developing a fine downy hair on the back; constipation.

Childhood-onset bulimia nervosa

At the age of 11, Kate had started boarding school and was very homesick. Soon after this, she found that she could stop herself from feeling sad and missing home by eating. She would eat a lot of food at one time (binge). Because she was worried that she would put on weight, she would make herself sick after she had binged. Kate became more and more worried about her weight and how she thought she looked, but said that she couldn't stop herself from bingeing and making herself sick even though she didn't get homesick any more. She said that she really hated herself. When Kate was seen for treatment, she was the normal weight for her height and age.

The telltale signs of bulimia nervosa can be divided into those that are related to food, those that are to do with general mood and behaviour, and those that are physical:

- *Food-related signs* – obsession with food; sensitivity about eating; wanting to eat alone; leaving the table during a meal or immediately after, often to go to the bathroom; collecting and storing food;

secretive eating; bingeing (see Glossary); denying hunger when it is obvious that they are hungry; drinking a lot of water (to make it easier to be sick).

- *General behaviour signs* – frequent weighing; excessive exercising; gathering information on dieting from leaflets, books and magazines; using laxatives; general irritability, especially when questioned about eating; developing rigid daily routines; not wanting to go out with friends anymore.

- *Physical features* – weight fluctuations, but generally around average weight; loss of, irregular or failure to start periods; dizziness, sometimes fainting; tiredness; mouth ulcers and tooth erosion; tension headaches.

Pervasive refusal syndrome

Milly had been referred for treatment from a paediatric ward at the age of 11, because she had been refusing food for three months. She also refused to walk, talk or take care of herself in any way. An examination found that there was no physical problem that would explain her symptoms and any attempts to help her were met with extreme resistance. Milly refused to take anything by mouth and so was fed by using a naso-gastric tube (see Glossary). During treatment it emerged that her father had a problem with alcohol and Milly had witnessed a number of violent attacks by him on her mother. Although, when questioned, she denied any sexual abuse, the results of the physical examination showed that this had occurred.

- This is a very serious condition.

- These children may refuse to walk, talk, eat, drink or take care of themselves in any way.

- There is no physical cause to explain the symptoms.

- These children are often very determined, angry or frightened.

- There is usually a history of conflict, violence and other problems within the child's family.

- It also appears that a history of sexual abuse contributes to this problem.

EATING PROBLEMS AND AGE GROUPS

The different types of eating problems affect children at different ages (see Table 1.1). For example, inappropriate texture of food for age is more commonly found in slightly younger children, while anorexia nervosa will usually affect slightly older children. The table below shows the different age groups at which the different types of eating problems are found. These have been divided into pre-school (0–5 years), primary school age (5–11 years) and adolescence (11–16 years).

Table 1.1   Summary of the types of eating problems

Eating problem	Pre-school	Primary school age	Adolescence
Inappropriate texture of food for age	✓✓	✓	✗
Food refusal	✓✓	✓	✗
Restrictive eating	✓✓	✓✓	✓
Selective eating	✓✓	✓✓	✓
Food phobia	✗	✓✓	✓
Food avoidance emotional disorder	✗	✓✓	✓
Pervasive refusal syndrome	✗	✓✓	✓
Childhood-onset bulimia nervosa	✗	✓	✓✓
Childhood-onset anorexia nervosa	✗	✓	✓✓

✓✓	disorder mostly found in this age group
✓	disorder sometimes found in this age group
✗	disorder does not occur in this age group

Things to remember

- The eating problems found in children are very different from the eating disorders that teenagers and adults suffer from.

- Eating problems in children are harder to identify than you might think, because there is still a lot of disagreement among professionals about the types of eating problems that children can suffer from.

- The types of eating problems that children can suffer from are:

    selective eating;
    restrictive eating;
    food phobia;
    food refusal;
    inappropriate texture of food for age;
    food avoidance emotional disorder;
    childhood-onset anorexia nervosa;
    childhood-onset bulimia nervosa;
    pervasive refusal syndrome.

two how many children suffer from eating problems?

It is important to know how many children suffer from eating problems so that we know how many children will need to be treated. Also, if we learn about the kinds of children who develop eating problems, then we may be able to find out what the risk factors are for developing eating problems in childhood. This in turn could help us to find ways to prevent children from developing eating problems in the first place.

WHAT DO WE KNOW?

When trying to work out how many children suffer from eating problems, professionals will look at figures on incidence. Incidence is the frequency with which a condition occurs in a population. To get precise incidence figures, large-scale studies need to be carried out. However, no large-scale studies have looked at children with eating problems, so the exact number of children who suffer from eating problems is not known.

Although there are no large-scale studies, the smaller-scale studies that have been carried out give us some information. Many of these studies have looked at children of pre-school age with eating problems. Some have investigated children from the general population, while others have looked at children with learning disabilities, physical disabilities or who have already been referred for treatment. The studies of children in the general population have found that:

- A third of children by the age of five years have had mild to moderate eating problems. Of this group, two-thirds suffer from selective eating and the other third from restrictive eating.

- Sixteen per cent of three-year-olds suffer from restrictive eating and 12% of three-year-olds suffer from selective eating.

- These eating problems are thought to last up to one year in about two-thirds of these children and up to five years in the other third.

- Seventy-one per cent of children under the age of one year are thought to continue to have a problem with eating until they are four years old.

The studies of children with a disability or who have already been referred for treatment have found that:

- A third of children with developmental delay (see Glossary) have been found to suffer from eating problems.

- Eighty per cent of children with severe learning disabilities are thought to suffer from eating problems.

- Children who suffer from cerebral palsy are thought to be more likely to have problems with eating because they tend to have problems with swallowing.

- Between 10% and 42% of children with chronic illnesses, such as kidney problems, liver disease, cystic fibrosis or cancer, are likely to suffer from eating problems.

- Of the children who had been referred for treatment at the eating problems clinic of Great Ormond Street Hospital, 78% were found to suffer from restrictive eating, 50% from inappropriate texture of food for age and 34% from selective eating (some children were given more than one diagnosis).

Another source of information on the number of children who suffer from eating problems is the professionals who treat the children. Professionals rarely treat children with food phobia, food avoidance emotional disorder or pervasive refusal syndrome, and bulimia nervosa in children is also quite rare. Most of the research that has investigated the numbers of children who suffer from anorexia nervosa has looked at children and adolescents together, so there is not much information on anorexia nervosa in children alone. Figures that have been reported for children between 10 and 14 years of age who suffer from anorexia nervosa are between 9.2 and 25.7 females per 100,000 of the population in a year. The figure for males is much less, at about 3.7 per 100,000 of the population in a year. It seems that professionals are much more likely to treat children who suffer from selective eating or restrictive eating than the other types of eating problems.

Eating problems seem to be quite common during the pre-school years, but there is not much information on how many children suffer from eating problems when they are of primary school age. There seem to be fewer children who suffer from eating problems between 8 and 13 years of age than there are between 14 and 19 years of age.

There are not very many services for children with eating problems, which may be because the demand for services for children with eating problems is not very high. More research is needed, however, so that we can find out exactly how many children have problems with their eating.

IS THE NUMBER OF CHILDREN WHO SUFFER FROM EATING PROBLEMS RISING?

At the moment there is a lot of disagreement about whether the number of children who suffer from eating problems is increasing. It might seem that more children are suffering from eating problems because, over the past ten years, more children are being referred for treatment of their eating problems. However, it could also be that:

- professionals such as doctors are now more aware that children can suffer from eating problems and so have begun to refer the children to specialist services for treatment;

  or

- both professionals and parents are now more aware that there are specialist services for children with eating problems and so are using them more.

It is difficult to answer the question of whether the number of children who suffer from eating problems is rising. This is because we need to know how many children suffer from eating problems in the first place to know if the number has increased. As we do not know the number of children who suffer from eating problems, we cannot say whether there are now more children with eating problems or not.

Things to remember

- The exact number of children who suffer from eating problems is not known.

- There seem to be fewer children with eating problems between the ages of 8 and 13 years than there are between the ages of 14 and 19 years of age.

- It is not known whether the number of children who suffer from eating problems is rising.

three what causes eating problems in children?

WHY DO SOME CHILDREN HAVE PROBLEMS WITH EATING?

What causes eating problems in children is a hard question to answer, but it is one of the most common questions asked by parents. The reason it is hard to answer is that we do not really know why eating problems develop in children. There is a lack of information because there has not been much research into the causes of eating problems in children. However, it seems likely that the eating problems that are found in children are not caused by just one factor, but by a number of factors that work together. These factors might be psychological, physical or to do with the family. Different factors are likely to play a part in the development of an eating problem at different times in the child's life. Some might have been there since the child was born, for example genetic factors, while others will play their part later on in the child's life, for example when the child goes to school.

There are three different types of factors that affect eating problems. These are called:

- predisposing factors;
- precipitating factors;
- perpetuating factors.

Some factors need to be present before the eating problem will develop. These are known as 'predisposing' factors, for example genetic factors or a particular type of personality. Other factors will cause the eating problem to start. These are called 'precipitating' factors. Examples of precipitating factors are puberty, family problems or problems at school. Finally, some factors will help the eating problem to carry on once it has started. These are known as 'perpetuating' factors. An example of a perpetuating factor is how the problem is managed.

In children of pre-school age, two different types of perpetuating factors (factors that maintain eating problems) have been found:

• those to do with the environment – for example, the child might not have been given the right types of food when he was younger or not given the right supervision and his behaviour not managed properly;

• those to do with physical problems that the child may have, for example with swallowing or gastro-oesophageal reflux (see Glossary).

Many children with eating problems have experienced physical difficulties when they were younger and these will have affected their early feeding as babies. When they get older and the physical problem has been cured, some children may still have problems with eating, not because of a physical problem, but because of a psychological problem. For example, if a child had to go into hospital because she kept on being sick when she was very young, then she might develop a fear that eating solid food would make her choke and be sick. She might therefore later on develop a food phobia.

Parent–child interactions will also have an effect on eating problems in children. For example, some children will cry, throw food, spit out food and push food away in order to get attention. Other children will refuse to eat, eat only a narrow range of foods or eat hardly anything at all because it is the only way in which they can have some control over their world. Often when children are worried about something or feel sad, they will use these behaviours so that they can show others how they feel. It is understandable that parents should be concerned and worried about their child's eating, and this can be worsened by pressure from health care professionals for the parents to ensure that the child is fed properly. Sometimes, however, children can pick up on these concerns, and this can cause the eating problem to last longer than it would otherwise have done. It is likely that mealtimes will end up being tense and unpleasant, and this can also maintain the problem.

ARE SOME CHILDREN MORE LIKELY TO SUFFER FROM EATING PROBLEMS THAN OTHERS?

There is little research that has investigated risk factors for the development of eating problems in children. However, a few research studies have found that some children are more likely to suffer from eating problems than others. Some studies have looked at risk factors that lead to the development of specific eating problems. These have found that:

- Some children who are slow feeders early on in their life seem to develop into restrictive eaters later on in childhood (they seem not to eat very much at all and are not interested in food).

- Some children who have had an unpleasant experience of feeding when they were young have been found to suffer from food refusal when they are older. They might have kept on being sick, choked or gagged on solid food or even had gastro-oesophageal reflux (see Glossary).

- Some children do not have a normal experience of eating when they are young; for example, they might have had long periods of naso-gastric feeding (see Glossary). This may cause the child to be frightened of tasting and eating new types of food. If this happens, then the child will not progress on to solid food and will suffer from inappropriate texture of food for age later on. Other children might not have learnt the skills needed to cope with solid food, and so again will eat only pureed food and not eat the appropriate texture of food for their age.

Other studies have looked at risk factors in general terms rather than investigating risk factors that may lead to specific eating problems. These studies have found that:

- Feeding problems are common in premature babies and babies of low birth weight.

- Children with eating problems have problems reaching motor milestones such as being able to sit upright, walking on their own and learning to be toilet trained. Also, some children with eating problems have been found to have a delay in being able to talk.

- Distress around feeding during the first three months of life is commonly reported by mothers of children with eating problems. Weaning also seems to have been a problem, with some children refusing to eat pureed baby food and others refusing lumpy baby food. Infants who have problems with feeding up to three months of age are more likely still to have a problem at three to six months. Also, children with eating problems at three to twelve months are more likely still to have a problem at four years of age.

- It seems that if children are regularly sick when they are younger, then they are more likely to have problems with eating when they get older. The parents of children referred to Great Ormond Street Hospital reported that 70% of their children had been sick regularly or frequently.

- There are more boys who suffer from childhood eating problems than the number of males who suffer from eating disorders as teenagers or adults. For example, it is thought that about 30% of children who suffer from anorexia nervosa are boys. This is much higher than the number of males who have eating disorders as teenagers or adults: the Eating Disorders Association states that between 5% and 10% of those with eating disorders are male.

- Most of the children who receive treatment for anorexia nervosa come from the higher social classes. It is thought that about half the children treated for anorexia nervosa are from a middle-class background. It is important to point out here, however, that this may not mean that childhood-onset anorexia nervosa is more likely to occur in middle-class children. It may be that these types of families are better at making use of the services open to them.

- Eating problems used to be found only in people who had a white ethnic origin. Now, however, professionals are treating children from other ethnic groups. In particular, they are starting to treat children from families who keep their own beliefs and practices and socialise only with others from the same racial origin.

Things to remember

- We do not really know why children develop eating problems.

- It is thought that there is more than one factor that causes eating problems in children.

- These factors will affect the child at different times in the child's life.

- It appears that some children are more likely to suffer from eating problems than others. For example, it seems that children are more likely to suffer with an eating problem if they:

   had an unpleasant, abnormal or slow early feeding experience;
   had a low birth weight;
   are delayed in their development;
   develop problems with eating early on in their lives;
   have a history of being sick.

---

four who treats children with eating problems?

Most children who have eating problems will not need to be seen by a professional for treatment. This is because their eating tends to become better with time. However, if children are referred for treatment for their eating problem, there are quite a few different professionals whom they could see and quite a few ways in which they could be treated. Children tend to receive different treatments depending on the eating problem that they have and the professional to whom they go for treatment. So who might your child see?

WHAT TYPES OF PROFESSIONALS TREAT CHILDREN WITH EATING PROBLEMS?

As already said, there are a number of different professionals who could be involved in the assessment and treatment of children with eating problems. These professionals include:

- community practitioners;
- nutritionists;
- psychologists;
- health visitors;
- nurses;
- psychiatrists;
- occupational therapists;
- speech therapists;

- physiotherapists;

- social workers.

These different types of professionals have been trained in different areas and so have special skills (they are described under separate headings, below). In practice, however, they may do similar sorts of things. For example, if a child has oral-motor problems (problems with the muscles that they need to use when they eat), then they could be treated by either a speech therapist or a physiotherapist. The type of professional who treats the child will depend on where the child is referred to.

Unfortunately, there are no clinical standards or guidelines that will tell you which professionals should treat a particular child or how the child should be treated. It is thought, however, that for treatment to be effective, professionals from different backgrounds will need to work together. Which professionals do become involved in treating a child will depend on:

- the type of eating problem;

- how bad the eating problem is;

- the clinical resources available;

- the organisation of health care services within the area;

- the background and practice of those managing the case.

Community practitioners

Feeding problems may first be uncovered through a routine check-up with a family doctor, through a community paediatrician (see Glossary) who is managing a child with an acute illness or through a visit to a GP because a parent is concerned about the child. The GP or community paediatrician may either try to treat the problem themselves or they may think it better to refer the child to a medical specialist, for example a paediatric gastroenterologist (see Glossary) to diagnose gastro-oesophageal reflux (see Glossary) or a radiologist to help to find out more about swallowing problems that the child may have. This will depend on the eating problem that the child has.

Nutritionists

Paediatric nutritionists will look at the nutritional status and diet of the child. They will try to find out what a parent knows about nutrition and the details of the family diet. They can provide parental counselling and may also consult with other professionals. They may treat children who have problems with their metabolism (see Glossary), lung disease or children with burns, for example.

Psychologists

Child psychologists will work with children and their families to improve the relationship between the child and parents. They will try to reduce the stress around mealtimes by designing ways to change the behaviour of both the child and the parents.

Health visitors

Health visitors are registered nurses trained in a health prevention role. They work within the community as members of the primary health care team and may also work as part of a local child and adolescent mental health team. They often assess and manage problems associated with behaviour, eating and sleep.

Nurses

Paediatric nurses often treat infants and young children who are in hospital, and they play an important part in monitoring the progress of feeding interventions. If the intervention is based in an outpatient setting, mental health nurses may provide counselling or they may coordinate services. Visiting nurses may also provide support actually in the home.

Psychiatrists

Child and adolescent psychiatrists will assess any emotional and behavioural problems of children and their families. They are also trained to be able to pick up on other diseases, particularly those due to problems with the development of the nervous system and diseases that are 'genetically determined' (see Glossary).

Occupational therapists

Paediatric occupational therapists will usually look at how children use their arms and hands when eating. They will position and teach children how to eat on their own. They may work individually with children but in addition show parents how to help children to eat on their own. They may also act as a consultant to other professionals.

Speech therapists

Paediatric speech therapists are specifically trained to evaluate whether a child has a problem with the muscles that are used when eating (such a problem is termed 'oral-motor dysfunction'). They will therefore treat children with problems in oral-motor activity or swallowing.

Physiotherapists

Physiotherapists are trained to understand how muscles develop and work. They will therefore treat children who have problems with eating because they cannot use their muscles properly, for example children with cerebral palsy.

Social workers

Social workers provide therapeutic services such as individual counselling for parents or family therapy. They will also sort out and coordinate community services if they are needed. Occasionally they may act as a case manager on a feeding team.

WHAT ABOUT SPECIALIST SERVICES FOR CHILDREN WITH EATING PROBLEMS?

There are very few specialist services that treat children with eating problems (although there are quite a few specialist units for adolescents). It has been noticed that children with eating problems may not present to an eating disorder specialist to begin with. One study found that 52% of children who had anorexia nervosa had spent time on a general paediatric ward before they were referred to a specialist child psychiatric team. It is thought that this is because some professionals are not aware that children can suffer from eating problems. This is especially true in the case of boys with eating problems.

Things to remember

- Most children who have eating problems will not need to be seen by a professional for treatment because they will simply grow out of their eating problem.

- If children do need treatment, however, they could be seen by any one of a large number of professionals.

- These professionals could be:

    community practitioners;
    nutritionists;
    psychologists;
    health visitors;
    nurses;
    psychiatrists;
    occupational therapists;
    speech therapists;
    physiotherapists;
    social workers.

- There are no standards or guidelines to tell you which professional should treat a particular child.

- There are hardly any specialist units that treat children with eating problems.

what type of treatment is available for children with eating problems?

It is important first to point out that most children who have problems with eating will not need to have treatment, as their eating will become better with time.

If you are worried about your child's eating or weight, however, then it is a good idea to get some professional advice. A professional will be able to give you the help and advice that you need, or even just reassure you that everything is OK. As a general rule, if medical opinion is that the child is growing normally and is happy and healthy, then the eating problem should be left well alone. This is because the child should simply grow out of the eating problem.

If you are worried about your child's eating, however, what should you do?

TO WHOM SHOULD YOU GO TO BEGIN WITH?

The first 'port of call' should be your family doctor or GP. You need to keep in mind that not all doctors have a specialist knowledge of eating problems, so they may not seem particularly responsive to your concerns. If this is the case, then you need to make sure that you give them a clear picture of what the problem is. Describe your child's eating behaviour but also his or her general behaviour, for example if you have noticed a change in his or her mood. The doctor may ask you a number of questions and ask to examine the child. During the examination the doctor may check the child's:

- weight;

- height;

- pulse;

- blood pressure.

The doctor may also:

- listen to the child's chest;

- feel the abdomen;

- check the skin colour.

The doctor may also want to do some tests, for example a blood test, or ask for a urine sample. This will be followed by an initial diagnosis. The doctor may say that the eating problem is 'just a phase' and that the child will 'grow out of it'. Although this is usually true for children of pre-school age, it is less likely to be true for older children.

If your child is of primary school age, you may therefore need to be persistent. This is because some doctors may feel that they do not have the knowledge needed to assess and manage eating problems in children properly, or may not have the time or the resources to do so. They usually will play a part only in the early stages of intervention, as they should refer the child to a specialist – perhaps a dietician, paediatrician, child psychologist, child psychiatrist, nurse, social worker, counsellor, psychotherapist or family therapist (see also Chapter 4). The ideal situation would be to get a referral to an eating disorders clinic that will treat children as well as teenagers, but this may not be possible as there are few specialist services for children with eating problems.

WHAT DOES SPECIALIST TREATMENT INVOLVE?

Once children with an eating problem have been referred to a specialist service, there are quite a few ways in which they can be treated. Children tend to receive different treatments depending on their eating problem. Treatment will also depend on which professional is treating them. One thing that does not change is that children need to be able to grow and develop normally. They need help in expressing how they feel so that they do not need to do it through their eating and food any more.

It is important that:

- you are involved in the treatment of the child;

- you agree about how the child is to be treated;

- there is lots of information available for yourself and other family members about the treatment and the child's eating problem.

Healthy eating patterns need to be re-established so that the child can gain weight if he or she needs to. Generally, some combination of family work, counselling for parents, and individual therapy for the child should be offered. If the child has a very serious eating problem and a very low weight, a decision needs to be made as to whether he or she needs to be taken into hospital. If the child is very ill, you may also have to decide what to do about school.

WHAT TYPES OF TREATMENT ARE AVAILABLE?

Many different types of treatment are available for children with eating problems, but a child would not receive them all. Some – for example, physical treatments such as naso-gastric feeding (see Glossary) for children with anorexia nervosa – are used only if the child has become very ill and has lost a lot of weight. The other types of treatment that are offered are: behavioural therapy, cognitive–behavioural therapy, psychotherapy, family therapy and counselling for parents (described below).

Behavioural therapy

This form of treatment is most commonly used with children of pre-school age. Generally, one of two behavioural techniques may be used, depending on the child: one treats children who do not have the skills that they need to be able to eat properly; the other is used when children have these skills but do not use them in the right way.

Treatment of children who do not have the proper eating skills

If a child does not have the skills to eat properly, then the therapist will have to teach them. There are different ways in which this may be done. One is a technique called 'shaping', where the therapist breaks down the behaviour into smaller parts and then teaches the child each of these parts in turn until he or she can carry out the whole task. When the child carries out the behaviour correctly he or she is given praise and rewards. 'Prompting' may also be used, particularly if the behaviours do not occur very often. Prompts can be instructions, gestures, or physically guiding the child. Another technique is called 'modelling'. Here the therapist tells the child to 'do this' and then shows the child what to do. If the child copies the therapist correctly, he or she is given praise and rewarded. This will make it more likely that the child will carry out the behaviour in the future.

Treatment of children who have the proper eating skills

Some children have the proper skills that they need to be able to eat properly but do not use them. In this case, the therapist will either have to try to make the right eating behaviour happen more often, or try to make the wrong eating behaviour happen less often.

When trying to increase the right eating behaviour, the therapist will use what is called 'positive reinforcement'. This means that when the child behaves in the right way, for example putting the food into his or her mouth rather than throwing it on the floor, he or she will be praised and might be given a reward. Once the child behaves in the right way more regularly, the therapist will slowly begin to praise and reward the child less often. This is so that the child will continue to show the right eating behaviour on his or her own, and in the end will not need to be praised or rewarded at all.

There are a number of ways in which a therapist can try to decrease the wrong eating behaviour, such as spitting out food. For example, food that the child does not like can be disguised with food that he or she does like, so is less likely to spit out. Or, if a child is spitting food out, another technique is to continue to feed the child, because although the child will continue to spit the food out at first, in time the behaviour will lessen until it does not happen at all. This is called 'extinction' of a behaviour.

Cognitive–behavioural therapy

Cognitive–behavioural therapy is useful when treating bulimia nervosa, selective eating and food phobia.

The idea of cognitive–behavioural therapy for children with an eating problem is to help them to look at the way they think and to try to identify how this is causing a problem with their eating. The therapist will be aiming for a change in the child's behaviour along with a change in the way that the child thinks. The first goal of therapy is to understand how thoughts and feelings are associated with the child's environment. The therapist will explain how thoughts can influence the way that a person feels in a particular situation and that certain behaviours will make a person think or feel a certain way.

Cognitive–behavioural therapists tend to use different techniques for treating children than they do for treating adults. For example, to begin with it is important to make people undergoing therapy understand that what they think about their world can affect how they feel, and that they can think different things about the same situation which will make them feel a different way. To do this adults are usually asked to write a diary of their thoughts, behaviours and feelings. This may be difficult for children to do, however, so they are encouraged to keep 'cartoon' diaries, using pictures and thought and speech bubbles to record the most important events of their day. Other techniques that are adapted for the treatment of children are the use of board games with cards that contain unfinished sentences about family, emotions, experiences and behaviour. This can help the child and therapist to test ideas about the issues underlying the child's eating problem. Another technique is called the 'worry bag': the child is given a picture of an outline of a bag and encouraged to draw his or her worries inside it. This lets the child know that it is okay to have worries and also makes the worries seem more real and easy to cope with. The worries that the child has can then be discussed at each session and ways of solving each worry can be worked out or tasks can be set to challenge the negative thoughts that the child has about what might happen.

Rewards can also play an important part in therapy. When treating adults or teenagers, token charts are used. However, when treating children, rewards need to be more visually rewarding, so pictures are usually used. These will gradually form as the child is rewarded. For example, children who have a food phobia can add a petal to a flower every time they try a new food, or children who suffer from selective eating can make a caterpillar get longer and longer by adding another body section each time they try a different type of food (see figure 5.1).

Psychotherapy

Psychotherapy is thought to be particularly useful when treating children who suffer from anorexia nervosa and food avoidance emotional disorder but is also used to treat children with bulimia nervosa and pervasive refusal syndrome.

It is important that individual work is carried out alongside counselling for parents or the family as a whole. Before starting individual therapy, family assessments are carried out so that the therapist can look at how members of the family relate to one another. An individual assessment is also carried out to find out about the history of the child.

It is important that a reliable and regular timetable of meetings is agreed, which helps the child to develop trust in the therapist. The idea of psychotherapy is to create an environment where:

- the child can feel safe;
- consideration is given to the experiences of the child;
- the child is accepted, even if destructive or rejecting;
- care and definite boundaries are provided.

Psychotherapists tend not to ask questions or make comments during therapy, but listen to what the children have to say. Afterwards they will try to give some meaning to what the children have said. Therapy tries to help children to feel understood and accepted, so that they can become stronger and be able to deal with their feelings in other ways than through their eating.

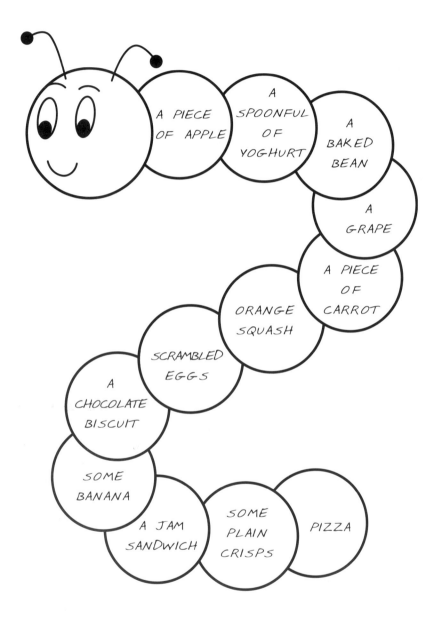

Figure 1.1 Cognitive–behavioural therapy tools: example of a picture reward chart for a selective eater. Each part of the caterpillar contains a description of a food type that can be added to the length of the caterpillar once the child has tried that particular type of food.

Family therapy and parental counselling

Family therapy and parental counselling is the only treatment approach to have been shown to be particularly effective in treating children with eating problems, even though we do not know which bits of this package of treatments are most important.

Family therapy focuses on the family as a whole rather than any individual members. Therapy looks at:

- how the adults act as parents;

- how the parents get on in their marriage;

- how close the children are to their parents;

- how protective family members are towards the child with the eating problem;

- how the family communicate.

The therapist will take a history of the family and look at what contributions the past might have made to the current problem.

Family therapy aims to improve the quality of parenting by helping the adults to start working together rather than against each other. It also aims to try to get the family to identify and acknowledge the problems and conflicts, and to find a way of resolving them. Some families need help to communicate properly and more constructively. There may be too much communication going on between family members or there may not be enough. Treatment will depend on the type of communication problem.

Physical treatments

Physical treatments are usually needed only in the more severe cases of eating problems, such as childhood-onset anorexia nervosa or food avoidance emotional disorder. These children have usually lost a lot of weight and need to be taken into hospital. They are often also dehydrated because they have not been drinking enough fluid.

To begin with, it is important to help the child to rehydrate and to put some weight on. Artificial feeding programmes are usually used in these extreme cases. Such programmes could be based on naso-gastric feeding (see Glossary), which involves passing a narrow tube down the nose into the stomach. The child is then fed via the tube with liquid food that is high in calories and nutrients.

Some of these children will also have other emotional problems, such as depression, and these are usually treated with medication.

WHAT SHOULD I DO IF MY CHILD HAS...?

Selective eating (extreme faddiness)

• The diets of most selective eaters, although restricted, will usually contain enough protein, carbohydrates, fat, vitamins and minerals so that the child will be healthy and grow normally.

• If the child is not upset or worried about eating, then there is little that you need to do. You should try to accept the narrow diet, expecting that it will become wider in time.

• If the child's diet has a high sugar content, then regular visits to the dentist will be needed.

• If you are concerned, then go to your family doctor or GP, who will check that the child is healthy and growing normally.

• The best time to offer treatment for selective eating is when the child wants it. Many of these children become embarrassed about their eating as they get older. This is because their eating problem is causing them difficulties with their friends. It is hard for them to stay at a friend's house or go to their friends' birthday parties because they are worried about what food will be available for them to eat.

• For children whose selective eating has had no physical effects, and who are healthy and growing normally, and who now want to be treated, a combination of parental counselling and individual therapy is offered.

- The individual therapy helps children to try new foods and to decide which foods they will try, how much of each new food, when and where they want to try it. Also, they will decide who they want to be there when they try the new food. To begin with children will try only a very small amount of one food. It is important that the trying of new types of food is taken at the pace of the child. This may mean that progress is very slow.

- Parental counselling will help the parents to make sure that they are consistent in the way that they try to help the child. It will also show them how to support the child by using praise and rewards and not forcing or punishing the child.

- Once a child is being treated for selective eating, you will need to be patient, as treatment may take time.

Restrictive eating (poor appetite)

- It is important to seek advice from a medical professional such as your family doctor or GP, who should check that the child is healthy.

- More often than not, however, there will be no physical problem that accounts for the small amount of food eaten.

- Generally, if the child is growing normally and is healthy, then there is no need to try to treat the restrictive eating of the child. This is because the child's appetite will usually increase with age.

- It is best to avoid encouragement, persuasion or force, as these make no difference and can make the eating problem worse.

- It is best to leave well alone if the doctor has said that no harm is being done to the growth and development of the child, because giving too much attention to the problem can make it worse.

- This will be the case for most children who suffer from restrictive eating.

- However, what if children's restrictive eating is having an effect on their growth and health? In this case they would be taken into hospital for treatment. Sometimes, doing this and changing the children's environment it is enough to make them eat more. If this does not make them eat more, they will still be at risk. If the child is very short, then growth hormones may be used, which will stimulate appetite and growth. It is important to note that these are used only as a last resort in treatment and that the majority of children who suffer from restrictive eating do not need treatment.

Food phobia

- It is advisable to seek professional help for this problem.

- It is not a good idea to try to persuade the child to eat, as this can make the problem worse.

- Treatment of this problem will depend on whether the child has a physical problem that has added to the food phobia and the specific fears that the child has about eating.

- If the child has a physical problem, then this will need a specific type of treatment. For example, if the child has gastro-oesphageal reflux (see Glossary), then medication will be used to speed up the emptying of the stomach; or if the child has difficulty in swallowing, then speech therapy may help the child to overcome this.

- Cognitive therapy is usually used to treat fears of taste, texture and being sick, choking or suffocating. This usually helps children to relax so that they are not so worried or anxious. The exact cognitive techniques that are used will depend on how old the child is.

- The most important thing as a parent is to have a lot of patience and perseverance.

Food refusal

- It is important to seek professional help because in older children food refusal is often a sign of underlying unhappiness or worries that the child has. These children refuse food because they find it difficult to express how they are feeling.

- Once the worries have been identified and worked upon, then they will tend to refuse food less often.

Inappropriate texture of food for age

- It is a good idea to seek professional help because this condition can cause some children to lose weight; it is therefore important to check the child's physical health.

- For a child who will not eat lumpy food, it is important gradually to introduce texture into the child's diet.

- This can be done by first reducing the amount of liquid in the pureed food, to make the mixture more solid.

- Once the child will eat this more solid mixture, try to mash the food instead of blending it.

- You can then try to get the child to eat chopped food instead of the mashed food.

- It is important that you approach this in a consistent and planned way so that the child can build up confidence.

- It is also a good idea to give these children soft finger food, such as cooked vegetables, soft bread and pasta, so that they can have control over their eating. In this way they can try solid food that will dissolve easily in their mouth.

Food avoidance emotional disorder

- Because this condition is usually the consequence of more generalised distress, and because some of these children lose a lot of weight, it is important to seek professional help, so that the underlying distress can be treated.

- It is important to remember that the child genuinely finds it difficult to eat and so pressurising the child will not work and may make the situation worse.

- The assessment and treatment of this eating problem are similar to those for childhood-onset anorexia nervosa (see below). The difference is that the children with food avoidance emotional disorder usually have depression, anxiety or obsessive–compulsive symptoms as well. Medication is therefore more likely to be used to treat these symptoms.

- The medication prescribed can cause side-effects such as an upset stomach, feeling drowsy or having a dry mouth. These will usually disappear after a week or two, however. Medication should not be used unless there are good reasons for doing so.

Childhood-onset anorexia nervosa

- It is important to seek professional help from a specialist.

- You need to expect that these children will not eat normally and that some will make themselves sick or will exercise excessively (or both).

- Also expect that the child will be resistant and there will be a lot of arguments. You will nonetheless need to discuss how to tackle these behaviours and agree on what to do. It is important to be consistent.

- It is also important to take control of the family's eating, making decisions about which foods to buy and cook and deciding how much is eaten, and so on.

- You need to make sure that you have enough information about the condition and how it will be treated.

- A decision will have to be made as to whether or not the child needs to be taken into hospital. This would be more likely for children who are of a particularly low weight for their height and age, those with low blood pressure, a slow pulse or poor circulation in the hands and feet, those who are constantly being sick or vomiting blood, and those who have signs of depression.

- During treatment a weight that the child needs to reach should be calculated and the child will need a programme of re-feeding.

- Family and parental counselling are usually offered and individual therapy for the child.

- Decisions will also need to be made about school.

Childhood-onset bulimia nervosa

- It is important to seek professional advice from a specialist.

- You need to help the child to have a more regular eating pattern, to avoid purging (see Glossary) and other behaviours to control weight gain, such as exercising, and to improve their low-self esteem.

- The treatment of bulimia nervosa involves working out an eating pattern that the child can follow. This is so that bingeing and purging (see Glossary) can be reduced.

- Family therapy and parental counselling, and individual therapy for the child should be offered, which give support and advice.

- Individual work carried out with the child is usually cognitive–behavioural therapy and helps to identify what is happening, when it happens, what triggers the compulsions (see Glossary) to binge and then purge. It also helps the child to work out ways in which to overcome these compulsions.

- Therapy also helps children to look at the negative thoughts that they have about themselves and to re-evaluate these to increase their self-esteem.

- In some cases medication is needed to help to reduce the urge to binge; if the child is also suffering from depression, then anti-depressants may be prescribed.

Pervasive refusal syndrome

- It is vital to seek professional help, as these children tend to become very ill indeed.

- Children suffering from pervasive refusal will need treatment at an inpatient psychiatric unit and their stay is likely to be anything from several months to one year.

- They will probably need to be fed using a naso-gastric tube (see Glossary). A combination of individual, group and family therapy is also usually needed and sometimes medication.

- These children are often very ill and it will take time for them to recover.

Things to remember

- Most children will not need treatment for their eating problem because it will get better with time.

- If you are worried about your child's eating, then it is a good idea to get professional help.

- Your GP or family doctor should be the first 'port of call'.

- If medical opinion is that your child's eating problem is not affecting growth and development and the child is happy and healthy, then it is best to leave well alone.

- If the eating problem is having an effect on the child's growth, then they will need treatment. The main types of treatment available are:

  behavioural therapy;
  cognitive–behavioural therapy;
  psychotherapy;
  family and parental counselling;
  physical treatment.

- The type of treatment that your child will receive will depend on the eating problem and which professional the child is referred to for treatment.

what is the long-term outlook for children with eating problems?

It is understandable that any parent who has a child with an eating problem will be worried about what the future holds. In fact, the long-term outlook for most children who suffer from eating problems is very good. This is because they tend to grow out of their eating problem, and the problem will not have caused them any harm.

Research into the outcome of eating problems in children is important so that better methods of treatment can be developed and predictions can be made about future outlook. Unfortunately, little such research has been done. Most of what we do know has come from the experience of professionals who treat children with eating problems.

The outlook will depend on the type of eating problem that the child has, whether it has caused the child to lose a lot of weight, and whether the experience has had an effect on the child's psychological well-being.

WHAT IS THE OUTLOOK FOR...?

Selective eating (extreme faddiness)

- Children who suffer from selective eating have a very good long-term outlook. By the time the children become teenagers, almost all of them will have grown out of selective eating.

- The children who do not grow out of it – probably less than 1% – will carry on to be selective eaters as adults. Selective eating does not seem to be such a problem to them at this age, however.

- There are no long-term consequences of selective eating regardless of whether the person has grown out of it or not.

Restrictive eating (poor appetite)

- Restrictive eaters tend to be poor eaters throughout their childhood but they have a good outlook. This is because their appetite seems to get bigger as they get older and by the time they are adults they are eating satisfactorily.

- Restrictive eaters tend to grow into thin adults but they are not unhealthy.

- Although these children are often underweight, this does not seem to cause them any physical problems because they seem to have naturally small appetites and so stay healthy.

- The only source of long-term distress for this eating problem is if the child has been pressurised into eating more.

Food phobia

- This is a rare condition so there is not much information on the long-term outlook for it.

- It is a difficult condition to overcome, but as there are even fewer adults than children who suffer from it, it seems likely that most children grow out of it.

- If the child has a very limited diet and has lost a lot of weight, then complications may be similar to those found in children with anorexia nervosa. These children may also have ongoing psychological problems if they have been pressurised into eating.

Food refusal

- Worry or unhappiness tends to underlie the food refusal in many cases.

- These children are usually of normal weight and height for their age, as this problem does not usually cause them any harm physically.

- For this reason, if the underlying worries and unhappiness are treated, then these children have a good outlook.

Inappropriate texture of food for age

- Inappropriate texture of food for age is more often found in younger children than in older children, which seems to suggest that this problem has a good outlook.

- Most of these children tend to be of normal weight and with treatment will gradually start to eat different foods that are more appropriate for their age.

Food avoidance emotional disorder

- There is not much information available about the long-term outlook of this disorder.

- If the correct treatment is followed and the children's emotional difficulties are treated, these children do tend to make a good recovery.

- It seems likely that recovery will be slow, as with the other eating problems.

- Long-term problems may occur if the child has lost a lot of weight, has been pressurised into eating or the child's emotional problems have not been resolved.

Childhood-onset anorexia nervosa

- Childhood-onset anorexia nervosa is a difficult eating problem to overcome and is probably the hardest of the eating problems for children to recover from. It also has the worst long-term outlook.

- About two-thirds of the children who suffer from anorexia nervosa make a good recovery, while a third only partly recover; 5% will remain unwell for a number of years and a small number will die.

- Death in children with anorexia nervosa is very rare and is usually due to the consequences of starvation, the effects of continuously making themselves sick or sometimes suicide.

- Recovery for children with anorexia nervosa is very slow. Most of the physical effects of starvation seem to reverse when the children gain weight and any long-term consequences can be treated.

Childhood-onset bulimia nervosa

- If they are treated by a specialist, the outlook for children who suffer from bulimia nervosa is quite good.

- It has been shown that cognitive–behavioural therapy is an effective treatment in adults because it helps the person to reduce bingeing (see Glossary) and purging (see Glossary). It is thought that cognitive–behavioural therapy is also a useful treatment for children, again to help them to eat normally and gradually stop bingeing and purging.

- Recovery will take time. Any long-term effects will be due to sufferers repeatedly making themselves sick or the use of laxatives (see Glossary), but these effects can be treated.

Pervasive refusal syndrome

- This is a rare condition and there has been no research into the outlook for it, so it is not known what the future holds for these children.

- They are often very ill and have lost a lot of weight. However, the children who have been seen have made progress, although this takes time.

- The key to a good outlook for these children is getting the professional help that they need from an in-patient psychiatric unit that has the resources to treat the child for a long period of time.

- More research is needed, however.

WHAT EFFECT CAN EATING PROBLEMS HAVE ON GROWTH AND DEVELOPMENT?

Physical well-being can be looked at in terms of a scale. At one end of the scale there are children who have normal weight, growth, development and eating patterns, and at the other end are children who suffer from illnesses such as anorexia nervosa that affect all of these things. Between these two extremes there are the children who suffer from the other types of eating problems. For example, bulimia nervosa affects metabolism (see Glossary) and the functioning of the hormones, eating patterns are disturbed and the child's weight may be low, normal or high. In a child with selective eating, however, weight, growth and development are usually not affected despite an extremely limited diet. Food avoidance emotional disorder can be found closer on the scale to anorexia nervosa because these children can lose a lot of weight, and this can have an effect on their growth and development.

It is important to remember that the effects on growth and development discussed here are not relevant for most children who suffer from eating problems. This is because their eating will become better in time without causing them any harm physically. The effects that will be discussed apply to only a very small number of children with eating problems. These children will have lost a lot of weight, in some cases so much so that their life is in danger.

Physical assessment

Children need to take in enough energy, protein and other essential nutrients so that they can grow and develop. It is important to be able to identify the effects that eating problems have on the body so that it is possible to distinguish a body that is starving from a body that is thin but normal. In order to be able to do this, a physical assessment needs to be performed. This should involve more than measuring just height or weight. To monitor the growth of a child effectively:

• suitable growth charts need to be available;

• correct measurement techniques need to be used;

• measurements need to be transferred to the growth charts properly;

• growth charts need to be interpreted correctly.

It is also important to get information on body muscle mass and fat reserves. In order to do this, the most commonly used measurements are body weight, height, triceps skin-fold thickness, and the circum-ference of the mid-arm muscle.

Body weight

If a child's health or growth is causing concern, then the child should be weighed. Body mass index charts have been published. These provide information on what a child should weigh at a particular height. This will give a rough idea as to whether the child is underweight or not and provides a good starting point.

Height

Children's height will normally increase rapidly during the first two years of life. After this it gradually slows down to a more constant rate until the child reaches puberty. The child's rate of growth may increase between the ages of six and eight years, called the mid-childhood growth spurt, but it is when the child reaches puberty that their main growth spurt occurs. After puberty growth is more or less completed.

A major influence on the final height of a child is genetics. It is important to remember that a child may be short simply because his or her parents are. If children suffer from eating problems before they have finished growing, then this can have serious consequences on their final height and bone density. The long-term effect of suffering from eating problems before children have finished growing is not known because there has been no research on this.

Skin-fold thickness

Skin-fold thickness measurements of the triceps are useful in children because they can predict whether the child is underweight for his or her height. Skin-fold thickness can also be used to predict the growth spurt during puberty.

Growth curves

As a rule, if a child grows less than 4 cm in any year, then you should seek professional help. It is possible to assess whether your child is growing normally by constructing what is called a growth curve. One measurement taken in isolation will not give you enough information. A pattern needs to be established that can then be compared with a growth chart.

In order to get a growth curve, three measurements need to be taken about 6 to 12 months after each other. The growth curve should then run parallel to what are called 'centile lines' on the growth chart (see Appendix for details on how to assess a child's growth potential fully). Growth charts are available from the Child Growth Foundation (see Chapter 7, 'Need more information?', for the address).

General effects on the body

It is important to stress that most children with eating problems are happy and healthy and that their eating problem does not cause them any physical harm. They continue to grow and develop normally and will eventually grow out of their eating problem. There are a small number of children whose eating problem does cause them physical harm, however. These children will have lost a lot of weight. What effect does losing a lot of weight have on a child's body?

Fat stores play an important part in the effects that starvation has on the body. The amount of fat within the body varies and is relatively low during childhood and usually at its peak during puberty. If a child is aged eight or nine years and has problems with eating, which has caused a lot of weight loss, then this happens at a time when the child's body does not have a lot of energy reserves.

When a body does not get enough food, it will try to conserve energy. This is done by limiting energy supply and blood flow to non-essential organs. Non-essential organs are areas such as the hands and feet, the stomach and gut, and the skin. This causes symptoms such as cold hands and feet, pale skin and weak pulses. The brain will be the last organ to be affected by a fall in blood flow. The body will also break down tissue so that it can get the energy that it needs to keep the essential organs working properly.

There are many different things that can happen to the body because of not eating a proper diet. For example, differences in electrolytes (see

Glossary) are commonly seen in anorexia nervosa. Glucose metabolism (see Glossary) is irregular during starvation and low blood glucose levels can be found. There are also increased levels of the enzymes found in the liver, which is a sign the fats found in the liver are being broken down. Eating problems also have an effect on endocrine function (see Glossary), preventing the glands that release hormones into the body from working properly.

This all sounds very complicated, but what effect does not eating a proper diet have on a child's growth, bone density and sexual development?

Growth

One of the most sensitive markers of illness in childhood is the rate of growth for age. Unfortunately, we do not know very much about the expected growth patterns in children with eating problems. This is particularly true in the case of boys. The fastest period of growth for girls is at about the age of 11 and for boys at about the age of 15. If children experience eating problems before these ages, then they will not have finished growing and there may be serious consequences for their final height and bone density (see below).

One study has looked at growth in 15 children with anorexia nervosa. It found that, in all of them, growth had stopped for about 13 months before they were admitted to hospital for treatment. Nine of the children started to grow again and caught up in height after treatment but two of the children did not. Unfortunately, there is no information available about the effect on growth of the other types of eating problems found in children.

Bone density

One of the concerns for children with eating problems is that they may develop 'osteoporosis' because their bone strength is developing at this time. When someone has osteoporosis, it means that they have a low bone mass and that their bones are very fragile. This means that their bones are more likely to break or crack.

Factors that affect bone density are genetics, race, nutrition, body weight, sex steroids, growth hormones and exercise. Anorexia nervosa affects the majority of these factors, which means that suffering from anorexia nervosa increases the likelihood of developing osteoporosis. Eating problems that cause children to lose a lot of weight can have an effect on puberty (see below). One study has found that men who had a delay in puberty had a reduced bone density later on in life when compared with men who did not have a delay in puberty. Bone density in the other types of eating problems in children has not specifically been studied.

Sexual development

Puberty begins at different ages for boys and girls. The average age for boys is 12 years and that for girls is 11½ years. The beginning of puberty for boys involves the growth of pubic hair and testicular enlargement, and for girls their breasts begin to develop. In boys the growth spurt occurs quite late during puberty, whereas in girls it can begin before there are any other physical signs.

Not eating a proper diet can cause a delay in the start of puberty; if puberty has already started, then it may cause puberty to stop. Some of the changes due to puberty can also reverse. For example, girls on a poor diet may have what is called 'primary amenorrhoea', where their periods do not start, or 'secondary amenorrhoea', where their periods started but then stopped. Both are signs that the endocrine system (see Glossary) is not working properly. This means that the glands that secrete hormones are not working properly, and will not produce enough sex steroids. Sex steroids are important for growth, the development of healthy bones and secondary sexual characteristics, and the workings of the reproductive system.

The heart

Starvation also has an effect on the heart. It can cause 'bradycardia', which is when a person has a pulse of less than 60 beats per minute. It is thought that this happens as a result of the heart having to compromise because it is not getting enough energy to work normally. If the body has been starved for a long time, then it is thought that the muscle in the heart will break down. This increases the likelihood of an abnormally low blood pressure (hypotension) and sudden alterations in the heart beat (arrhythmias).

Liver and kidneys

Low fluid intake, being sick and using diuretics (see Glossary) can lead to dehydration and kidney stones. Kidney failure was seen in one 16-year-old because of muscle breakdown due to starvation. Fatty infiltration of the liver is well recognised in states of severe malnutrition.

The brain

The effect of anorexia nervosa or the other eating problems found in children on the developing brain is not known. Abnormalities in the structure of the brain have been seen on the brain scans of patients with anorexia nervosa. These abnormalities can partly reverse when the child gains weight. It is thought that in younger children they will fully reverse, but more investigation is needed.

Things to remember

- The long-term outlook for most children with eating problems is very good because they will grow out of their eating problem.

- For most children, their eating problem will not cause them any physical harm – they will grow and develop normally, and be happy and healthy.

- The exact outlook for children with eating problems will depend on the type of eating problem that they have and whether the eating problem has caused them to lose a lot of weight.

- For the very few children who do lose a lot of weight, their growth, bone density, sexual development, heart, liver and kidneys and brain could all have been affected.

- It is important to remember, though, that this is relevant only to children who have lost a lot of weight and not the majority of children with eating problems.

need more information?

If you need more information then there are lots of places that you can go to get it.

USEFUL ADDRESSES

Here is a list of addresses of organisations that should be able to give you more information, help and advice.

National Children's Bureau
8 Wakely Street, London EC1V 7QE
Tel: 020-7843-6000
http://www.ncb.org.uk

YoungMinds
102–108 Clerkenwell Road, London EC1M 5SA
Tel: 020-7336-8445
http://www.youngminds.org.uk

The Children's Society
The Edward Rudolf House, 69–85 Margery Street, London WC1X 0JL
Tel: 020-7841-4400
http://www.the-childrens-society.org.uk

The Child Growth Foundation
2 Mayfield Avenue, Chiswick, London W4 1PW
Tel: 020-8994-7625
http://www.cgf.org.uk

Department of Psychological Medicine (for children aged 2–15 years)
Great Ormond Street Hospital for Sick Children, Great Ormond Street, London WC1N 3JH
Tel: 020-7405-9200

Eating Disorders Research Team (for children aged 7–17 years)
Department of Psychiatry, Jenner Wing, St George's Hospital Medical School, Cranmer Terrace, London SW17 0RE
Tel: 020-8725-5514

Eating Disorders Service (for children aged 7–17 years)
Harewood House, Springfield University Hospital, Glenburnie Road, London SW17 7DJ
Tel: 020-8682-6751

FURTHER READING

If you prefer you can read on. The following books may be of use.

Bryant-Waugh, R. & Lask, B. (1999) *Eating Disorders: A Parent's Guide*. London: Penguin Books.

Fox, C. & Joughin, C. (2002) *Childhood-Onset Eating Problems: Findings From Research*. London: Gaskell.

Hirshmann, J. & Zaphiropoulos, L. (1993) *Preventing Childhood Eating Problems*. Carlsbad, CA: Gurze Books.

Lask, B. & Bryant-Waugh, R. (2000) *Anorexia Nervosa and Related Eating Disorders in Childhood and Adolescence*. Hove: Psychology Press.

how to assess a child's
growth potential

ADULT HEIGHT POTENTIAL

The adult height, which a child should expect to achieve genetically if his or her growth is absolutely normal, is called the mid-parental height (MPH). This is usually referred to in terms of one of the printed centiles on the centile chart – the mid-parental centile (MPC). Children may not always follow their mid-parental centile exactly, but all should grow within specific centiles, called their target centile range (TCR).

Calculation of a boy's mid-parental height/mid-parental centile

In order to calculate the MPH/MPC of a boy, it is important to know the height of both parents of the child. To give an example, the MPH/MPC of a boy whose father is 176 cm tall and whose mother is 160 cm tall would be calculated as follows:

(a) First, add the height (in centimetres) of the father to the height (in centimetres) of the mother: 176 cm + 160 cm = 336 cm.

(b) Divide your answer by 2:   336 cm/2 = 168 cm.

(c) Add 7 cm to your answer: 168 cm + 7 cm = 175 cm.

(d) 175 cm is his MPH – this can now be marked on a growth chart to the right of the 18-year line found on the horizontal axis (see Fig. 1).

(e) His MPC is the printed centile found on the growth chart nearest to his MPH – in this example this would be the 50th centile.

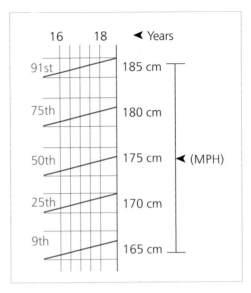

Fig. 1 Diagram to illustrate part of a growth chart for a boy (blue diagonal lines are centiles)

(f) His TCR is bordered by the two centiles 10 cm above and 10 cm below his MPH – that is, between the centiles found on the growth chart at 185 cm and 165 cm. In this case, therefore, his TCR is between the 91st centile and the 9th centile. This means that he should be growing within these two centiles from the age of 2 years.

Calculation of a girl's mid-parental height/mid-parental centile

In order to calculate the MPH/MPC of a girl, it is important to know the height of both parents of the child. To give an example, the MPH/MPC of a girl whose father is 186 cm tall and whose mother is 156 cm tall would be calculated as follows:

(a) First, add the height (in centimetres) of the father to the height (in centimetres) of the mother: 186 cm + 156 cm = 342 cm.

(b) Divide your answer by 2:   342 cm/2 = 171 cm.

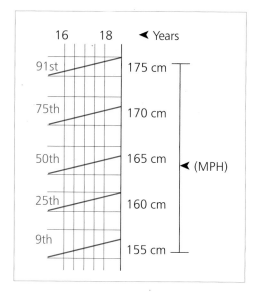

Fig. 2 Diagram to illustrate part of a growth chart for a girl (blue diagonal lines are centiles)

(c) Subtract 7 cm from your answer: 171 cm – 7 cm = 164 cm.

(d) 164 cm is her MPH – this can now be marked on a growth chart to the right of the 18-year line found on the horizontal axis (see Fig. 2).

(e) Her MPC is the printed centile found on the growth chart nearest to her MPH – in this example this would be the 50th centile.

(f) Her TCR is bordered by the two centiles 8.5 cm above and 8.5 cm below her MPH – that is, between the centiles found on the growth chart at 172.5 cm and 155.5 cm. In this case, therefore, her TCR is between the 91st centile and the 9th centile. This means that she should be growing within these two centiles from the age of 2 years.

The addition or subtraction of 7 cm is to compensate for the average difference between the heights of Caucasian (White) men and women.

For further details, contact The Child Growth Foundation (see Chapter 7).

glossary

Binge/bingeing

Eating a larger amount of food in a short period of time than most people would eat under similar circumstances.

Compulsion

A compulsion makes a person act against their own wishes.

Developmental delay

Developmental delay means that a child has not reached the developmental milestones that are expected. For example, the child may start to walk or talk later than would usually be expected.

Diuretics

Diuretics are drugs that cause an increase in the excretion of urine.

Electrolytes

An electrolyte is a solution or a substance in solution that consists of various chemicals that can carry electric charges. Electrolytes can be found in the blood as acids, bases and salts, for example sodium, calcium, potassium, and magnesium.

Endocrine system

The endocrine system refers to glands that produce hormones inside the body. What they produce is distributed through the body by the bloodstream.

Failure to thrive	This term is used to describe infants who are not growing and developing normally; they have poor physical development.
Gastro-oesophageal reflux	This refers to a condition where the gastric contents of the stomach return to the oesophagus. Sometimes gastric contents return to the mouth and cause regurgitation and vomiting.
Genetically determined	This means that something is hereditary, that characteristics have been biologically transmitted from a parent to the child. For example, a child will inherit height, hair colour, size and shape from the parents.
Glucose metabolism	Glucose is a sugar that provides the tissues of the body with energy. Glucose metabolism describes the process by which glucose is changed into a form that the body can use for energy.
Laxatives	A laxative is something that causes the bowels to empty.
Metabolism	This describes the energy and material transformations that occur in living cells.
Naso-gastric feeding	This involves passing a narrow tube into the stomach via the nose. Feeding then occurs via the tube with specially prepared liquid food high in calories and nutrients.
Paediatric gastro-enterologist	A paediatric gastroenterologist specialises in children's stomach and intestinal diseases.

Paediatrician

A paediatrician is a doctor who specializes in the treatment of children.

Purge/purging

To purge is to eliminate the contents of the stomach and intestines, either by vomiting or by abusing laxatives (see above).

index

COMPILED BY LINDA ENGLISH

Page numbers in *italics* refer to figures and tables

adult height potential 53–55
  (appendix)
age groups affected by eating
  problems 10, *10*, 14
amenorrhoea (absence of periods)
  8, 9, 49
anorexia nervosa, childhood-onset
  see childhood-onset anorexia
  nervosa
anxiety 5, 7, 36, 37
appetite, poor *see* restrictive eating
artificial feeding programmes 34
assessment
  by family doctor 26–27
  of growth potential 53–55
    (appendix)
  physical 45–47

behavioural therapy 28–29
bingeing 8, 9, 39, 44, 56
body, effects on 47–50
body mass index charts 46
body weight *see* weight loss;
  weight monitoring
bone density 48–49
books about eating problems 52
boys 14, 19, 25, 48, 49, 53–54
  (appendix)
bradycardia 49

brain, effects on 50
bulimia nervosa, childhood-onset *see*
  childhood-onset bulimia nervosa

cartoon diaries 30
causes of eating problems 16–20
cerebral palsy 13, 24
child and adolescent psychiatrists 23
childhood-onset anorexia nervosa
  7–8, *10*
  in boys 14, 19
  food-related signs 8
  general behaviour signs 8
  long-term outlook 43–44
  numbers of children treated
    13–14
  physical effects 8, 44–45,
    47–48, 49, 50
  referral to specialist services
    24–25
  risk factors 19
  treatment 28, 31, 33, 38
childhood-onset bulimia
  nervosa 8–9, *10*
  food-related signs 8–9
  general behaviour signs 9
  long-term outlook 44
  physical effects 9, 45
  treatment 30, 31, 38–39, 44

child psychologists 23
choking, fear of 4–5, 36
chronic illness 13
classification of eating problems
    2–3
cognitive–behavioural therapy
    30–31, 32, 39, 44
cognitive therapy 36
community paediatricians 22
community practitioners 21, 22
compulsions 39, 56

death 43
dehydration 33–34, 50
depression 7, 34, 37, 38, 39
development, effects on 44–50
developmental delay 13, 19, 56
disabled children 13

eating disorders clinics 27
eating disorders in adolescents and
    adults 1
eating skills problems, treatment
    for 29
electrolytes 47–48, 56
emotional problems 6–7, 34,
    37–38, 43
endocrine system 48, 49, 56
energy conservation 47
ethnic origin 20
extinction 29
extreme faddiness see selective
    eating

faddy eating see selective eating
family assessments 31
family doctors 22, 26–27
family problems 9
family therapy 33, 38, 39
fat stores 47
feeding problems in early life 18, 19

food avoidance emotional disorder
    6–7, 10
    effects on growth and
        development 45
    long-term outlook 43
    treatment 31, 33, 37–38
food phobia 4–5, 10
    causes 17
    long-term outlook 42
    treatment 30, 31, 36
food refusal 5–6, 10
    long-term outlook 42–43
    risk factors 18
    treatment 36

gastro-oesophageal reflux 18, 22,
    36, 57
general population, eating
    problems in 12–13
general practitioners (GPs) 22, 26–27
genetically determined diseases 23
girls 14, 48, 49, 54–55 (appendix)
glucose metabolism 48, 57
growth and development, effects
    on 44–50
growth charts 45, 47, 54 (appendix),
    55 (appendix)
growth curves 46–47
growth hormones 36
growth monitoring 45–47
growth potential, assessment of
    53–55 (appendix)

health visitors 21, 23
heart, effects on 49–50
height monitoring 46–47
hospital admission 28, 33–34, 35,
    38

identification of eating problems
    2–3

inappropriate texture of food for
    age 6, *10*
        long-term outlook 43
        numbers of children affected 13
        risk factors 18
        treatment 37
incidence studies 12–14
increase in eating problems,
    possibility of 14–15
individual therapy 31, 34–35, 38, 39
information, additional 51–52
in-patient psychiatric units 39, 44

kidneys, effects on 50

laxatives 9, 44, 57
liver, effects on 48, 50
long-term outlook 41–50
low birth weight 19

malnutrition, physical effects of
    47–50
medication 34, 36, 37–38, 39
mental health nurses 23
metabolism 45, 48, 57
middle-class background 19
mid-parental centile (MPC) 53–55
    (appendix)
mid-parental height (MPH) 53–55
    (appendix)
modelling 29

narrow range of foods *see* selective
    eating
naso-gastric feeding 18, 28, 34,
    39, 57
new foods, unwillingness to try 3,
    18, 31, 35
numbers of children with eating
    problems 12–15

nurses 21, 23
nutritionists 21, 23

occupational therapists 21, 24
oral–motor dysfunction 22, 24
organisations, addresses of 51–52
osteoporosis 48–49
outlook, long-term 41–50

paediatric gastroenterologists 22, 57
paediatricians 22, 58
paediatric nurses 23
paediatric nutritionists 23
paediatric occupational therapists 24
paediatric speech therapists 24
parental counselling 33, 34, 35,
    38, 39
parent–child interactions 17–18, 23
periods, absence of 8, 9, 49
perpetuating factors 16, 17
pervasive refusal syndrome 9, *10*,
    31, 39, 44
phobia about food *see* food phobia
physical assessment 45–47
physical effects of eating problems
    8, 9, 47–50
physical problems 17, 36
physical treatments 28, 33–34
physiotherapists 22, 24
positive reinforcement 29
precipitating factors 16–17
predisposing factors 16
premature babies 19
pre-school aged children *10*,
    12–13, 17
primary amenorrhoea (absence of
    periods) 49
primary school aged children *10*,
    14, 27
professionals
    disagreement among 2
    increased awareness in 14

numbers of children treated by
13–14
types involved in assessment and
treatment 21–24
prompting 29
psychiatrists 21, 23
psychologists 21, 23
psychotherapy 31
puberty 46, 49
purging 39, 44, 58

refusal of food *see* food refusal;
pervasive refusal syndrome
restrictive eating (poor appetite) 4, *10*
long-term outlook 42
numbers of children affected 12,
13, 14
risk factors 18
treatment 35–36
rewards 30–31, *32*
risk factors 18–20

school, refusal to eat at 5–6
secondary amenorrhoea (absence
of periods) 49
selective eating (extreme faddiness)
3–4, *10*
long-term outlook 41–42, 45
numbers of children affected
12, 13, 14
treatment 30, 31, *32*, 34–35
severe learning disabilities 13
sex steroids 49
sexual abuse 9
sexual development 49
shaping 29
skin-fold thickness measurement 46
slow feeders 18
social class 19
social workers 22, 24

solid food, refusal of 6, 18, 37
specialist services 24–25
numbers of children referred 14
what treatment involves 27–28
speech therapists 21, 22, 24, 36
spitting out of food 29
starvation, physical effects of 44,
47–50
sugary diet 4, 34
swallowing difficulties 13, 22, 24,
36

target centile range (TCR) 53
(appendix)
terms used for eating problems 2
texture of food *see* inappropriate
texture of food for age
treatment 26–40
numbers of children referred 14
specialist services 24–25, 27–28
for specific eating problems
34–39
types available 28–34
types of professionals involved
21–24
usually not needed 26
who to go to initially 26–27
triceps skin-fold thickness 46
types of eating problems 1–11
age groups affected 10, *10*
identification of 2–3
risk factors for 18

vomiting 8, 17, 19, 44

weaning 19
weight loss 8, 33, 45, 47–50
weight monitoring 46
worry bag 30